From Your Friends at **The MAILE**

COMPREHENSION CONNECTIONS

Build Comprehension Skills With Science & Social Studies Passages

Grade 1

Project Editor
Amy Erickson

Writers
Rebecca Brudwick, Lisa Buchholz, Mary Sue Chatfield,
Erin Harp, Linda Morgason

Editors
Deborah T. Kalwat, Mary Lester, Scott Lyons, Leanne Stratton

Art Coordinator
Donna K. Teal

Artists
Pam Crane, Teresa R. Davidson, Theresa Lewis Goode, Nick Greenwood,
Clevell Harris, Kimberly Richard, Greg D. Rieves, Rebecca Saunders,
Barry Slate, Donna K. Teal

Cover Artists
Nick Greenwood, Clevell Harris, Kimberly Richard

www.themailbox.com

©2000 by THE EDUCATION CENTER, INC.
All rights reserved.
ISBN #1-56234-425-0

Manufactured in the United States
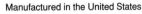
10 9 8 7 6 5 4 3 2 1

TABLE OF CONTENTS

MAKING CONNECTIONS

What's the key to comprehension? Connections! Connections between words and meanings, between text and concepts, and between text and prior knowledge. Not only do these connections help students understand what they read, but they help them recall it, too!

Most students do not make these connections on their own, though. They need to be taught how. Learning a variety of strategies that they can use before, during, or after reading helps youngsters make these links and boosts comprehension.

> **Choose from among the tried-and-true strategies described here to match your students' needs. They're perfect for promoting comprehension of the passages in this book and of countless other reading materials!**

Before Reading

What do students already know about a topic? What misconceptions do they have? What experiences have they had with the concepts? The answers to these questions all relate to prior knowledge—the information and experiences that a student brings to a reading situation.

> Prior knowledge has a tremendous impact on comprehension because readers combine information from text with what they already know in order to gain meaning. Tap into prior knowledge and increase comprehension with the quick and easy ideas below.

- **It's in the Cards!:** Invite students to brainstorm words related to the reading topic. Write each word on a separate card. Ask students to group the cards and to explain their reasoning. If desired, post the grouped cards on a board. After youngsters read the text, have them revisit the groupings and make changes as appropriate to reflect the information they learned.

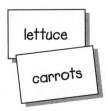  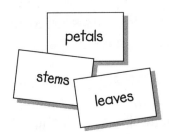

- **Set a Purpose:** Guide each youngster in setting a purpose for reading, such as finding the answer to a question or finding the most important sentence in a passage.

- **Take a Look!:** Encourage students to read the title and look at the illustrations. Then have them share their observations and tell what they wonder about the text.

During Reading

Does it make sense? This all-important question is one that good readers frequently ask themselves. In fact, they constantly self-monitor their reading. Use these ideas to heighten students' awareness of their comprehension as they read:

Frogs and toads don't chew? Wow! I wonder how they eat then. I'll keep reading and see if it says.

- **Think-Alouds:** Model this strategy by sharing your thought processes as you read aloud, interrupting your reading to verbally insert your predictions, context clues that you use, things you're wondering about…in short, any thoughts you have about the text. As you resume your reading, model how you pick up the train of thought where you left off. After several demonstrations, have students try the strategy in small groups.

- **Partner Up!:** This idea works well for multiparagraph passages. Pair students. One student in each pair reads the first paragraph to his partner. The listener summarizes the paragraph. The partners switch roles and then continue reading and summarizing the rest of the passage.

- **Stop and Restate:** Encourage each student to read a passage in small sections, stopping after each section to silently restate what he has read. If he has trouble restating at any point, he rereads the relevant section.

After Reading

So what was the passage about? Do you agree with the author? Continue the reading process with questions like these to help students fully understand the text. Here are some other effective follow-ups:

- **Picture-Perfect:** As soon as students finish reading a passage, invite them to describe any pictures they made in their heads as they were reading.

- **In Search Of:** Ask students literal and inferential questions about the passage. Have them determine whether each answer is "right there" in the passage, whether they need to "read between the lines" to find it, or whether they need to use their own opinions and experiences to answer.

- **Graphic Organizers:** Have youngsters organize and process the information they learned from reading by having each one use a copy of a provided graphic organizer (see pages 60 and 61) or inviting them to make their own webs and charts. For a whole-class follow-up, make a transparency of a graphic organizer and complete it with students.

ABOUT THIS BOOK
Overview

It's no secret that time is a precious commodity for teachers. So why not maximize it (and student learning!) by reinforcing reading skills and content area concepts at the same time? This book will help you do exactly that. Each comprehension unit is based on common science or social studies standards. Because each unit is three pages long, students have multiple opportunities to read about the same topic or theme. This repeated exposure helps them build prior knowledge and further strengthens comprehension.

Most text lends itself to practice with a few different comprehension skills. The passages in this book are no exception. The most significant skills on each page are indicated at the top of it.

Before Students Start

The words below are used in student directions in this book. For best results, familiarize students with the words before assigning any pages that include them.

- ***Passage:*** Explain that a passage is a piece of writing—not a story.
- ***Thoughts*** and ***Ideas:*** Many of the questions in this book ask students to write their thoughts or ideas. Point out that there is no one right answer for any of these questions, but that students should be able to support their reasoning.
- ***Column:*** Tell students that one way to organize words is by placing them in labeled columns, grouped under the appropriate headings.

In Every Unit

- **Prior Knowledge Question:** A question above each passage helps you set the stage for students' reading.

- **Words to Know:** Critical vocabulary words are noted. To introduce a word, try one or more of these ideas:
  — Discuss any multiple meanings.
  — Help students use familiar word parts to determine the word and its meaning.
  — Demonstrate what the word means; show the item it names or a picture of it.
  — Have students predict the meaning and an appropriate use of the word by dictating a sentence for it. Ask them to read the passage to check their ideas and then revise the sentence if needed.

chrysalis

- **Passage:** Each passage is designed for students who are reading on a mid- or late-first-grade level. Encourage students to read it more than once to increase fluency and, as a result, comprehension. Some students may benefit from using line markers to keep their place as they read.

- **Brain Builder:** A question for each passage promotes reflection and higher-level thinking. Use it as part of the assignment rather than as a bonus in order to ensure that all students have rich, thought-provoking experiences with the text.

How can you tell if something is living?

It's Alive!

How are boys, girls, rabbits, and trees the same? They are all alive! All living things need air, food, and water. Many of them need sunlight, too. Living things grow. A lot of them change as they grow.

A fish is alive. It needs air. It breathes through gills under the water. A tree is a living thing. It needs sunlight to make food. A person is alive. A person needs to drink water to be healthy. When living things get the things they need, they grow just as you do!

Words to Know
change
breathes
healthy

1. **Look** back at the passage. **Underline** the sentence that tells three things that living things need.

2. **Read** the words below. **Circle** the living things.

   water   people   rocks

   bugs   toys   trees

3. **Read** each question. **Circle** yes or no.
   a. Do fish need air?   yes   no
   b. Can a rabbit live without water?   yes   no
   c. Do all living things stay the same as they grow?   yes   no

On the back of this sheet, draw three living things. Write how you know they are living.

Brain Builder

How are living and nonliving things different?

Words to Know
reproduce   seeds
            smooth

Living or Nonliving?

Look around you. Everything you see is living or nonliving. How can you tell which things are alive? Keep reading to find out!

Living things need air, water, and food. They make new living things in different ways. People and animals have babies. Plants grow seeds. All living things grow. Some change as they grow.

Nonliving things are not living. They do not need air, water, or food. They cannot grow or reproduce. Some nonliving things can change with help. Wind can help a rock change. It can make it smooth.

Now you can tell living from nonliving things!

1. **Write** three things that living things need.

   _____   _____   _____

2. What does "nonliving" mean? _____

   _____

3. **Circle** yes or no.

   a. Nonliving things reproduce.   yes   no

   b. Living things grow.   yes   no

   c. A rose in a garden is a living thing.   yes   no

   d. Nonliving things need air and water.   yes   no

Brain Builder

On the back of this sheet, write two ways living and nonliving things are different.

What does it mean to grow?

Words to Know
change
care
young

Grow, Grow, Grow!

You can do a lot of things that you could not do when you were younger. That is because people grow and change. At first, people are babies who need a lot of care. They need to be fed. They cannot walk or talk. As babies grow, they learn to eat, walk, and talk alone.

Other living things grow and change, too. Animals are born as babies. They need to be fed and cleaned. As they grow, they learn to take care of themselves.

Plants also grow and change. They start as seeds. Then they grow roots, stems, and leaves. The plants get taller. Living things everywhere grow, grow, **grow!**

---

1. **Complete** each sentence with a word below. You will not use one word.

    seeds   care   learn   cannot

    a. Babies and young animals need a lot of _____.

    b. Plants begin as _____.

    c. Some living things _____ to do new things as they grow.

2. **Look** back in the passage. **Circle** the word that means "not with other people."

3. **Think** about the passage. How do people change as they grow?

    _____

    _____

> How are people and plants alike? How are they different? Write your ideas on the back of this sheet.

Brain Builder

What do plants need to grow?

Words to Know
air
light
soil

Growing Needs

What is green and can breathe, drink water, and eat? A plant can! Plants need air, water, and food. They need light, too. Plants take in air through holes in their leaves. Sometimes they get water from rain. Sometimes they get water from people. Plants drink the water through their roots. Many plants make their own food. They use light from the sun to make it. Plants get food from soil, too.

1. This passage is mostly about _____
   _____.

2. **Use** a yellow crayon. **Underline** the word in the passage that tells one thing that gives light to plants.

3. **Use** a brown crayon. **Underline** the word in the passage that means almost the same as "dirt."

4. **Look** back in the passage. What four things do all plants need?

   _____   _____   _____   _____

Brain Builder

Make believe that you work in a plant store. On the back of this sheet, make a poster that tells how to care for plants.

Name _____

What are the parts of a plant?

Words to Know
roots   stem   leaves

Plants come in many colors, shapes, and sizes. Many plants have three main parts. The parts are the roots, the leaves, and a stem. Some plants have flowers, too. Flowers make seeds for new plants. Roots hold a plant in the soil. Most roots grow under the ground. Leaves grow from a stem. The leaves make food for the plant. Some leaves are smaller than your thumb. Some leaves are much bigger than you!

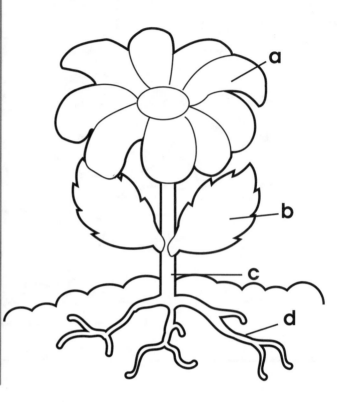

1. What is a good title for this passage? Why? _____
_____
_____

2. **Look** back in the passage. **Circle** the word that tells how many parts most plants have.

3. **Read** the words below. **Look** at the picture. **Write** the correct letters.

root ____   leaves ____   flower ____   stem ____

How are most plants alike? How are they different? Write your ideas on the back of this sheet.

Brain Builder

Name_____

Why do people need plants?

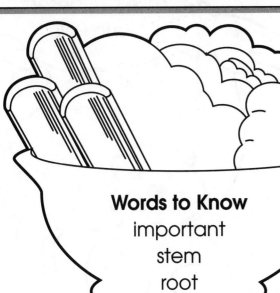

Words to Know
important
stem
root

Please Pass the Plants!

Plants are not just pretty. They are important, too! People need plants. Parts of many plants give people food. Yellow corn comes from the seeds of a plant. Green lettuce comes from the leaves of a plant. Red apples are fruit. Green celery is a stem. People can eat the roots of some plants, too! Roots like orange carrots are good to eat. Foods from plants help people grow and be strong.

1. **Look** in the passage. **Draw** a line to match each food with the plant part.

   corn •   • stem
   carrot •   • seed
   lettuce •   • fruit
   celery •   • leaves
   apple •   • root

2. **Read** each sentence. **Circle** yes or no.

   a. Carrots grow above the ground.
      yes   no

   b. Celery grows above the ground.
      yes   no

3. **Look** back at the passage. **Color** the picture to match the passage.

Brain Builder

Think about the passage. On the back of this sheet, draw a picture that shows why plants are important.

What do you know about mammals?

Words to Know
alike   desert
North Pole

Many Mammals

A mammal is a kind of animal. Dogs and bears are mammals. You and your friends are, too! All mammals are alike in three ways. They are warm-blooded. That means the air or water around them does not make their blood warmer or colder. A baby mammal drinks milk from its mother. Mammals have hair or fur.

Mammals live in many places. Camels live in the desert. Polar bears live near the North Pole. Whales live in the water. Rabbits spend a lot of time under the ground. Bats spend a lot of time in the air. You can see mammals all over the world!

1. **Look** back in the passage.
    a. **Use** a blue crayon to **underline** the mammals that live in the water.
    b. **Use** a green crayon to **underline** the mammals that fly.
    c. **Use** a brown crayon to **underline** the mammals that live under the ground.

2. **Read** the words below. **Draw** a line from each mammal to one place you might see it.

camel	•	• North Pole
polar bear	•	• sky
whale	•	• desert
bat	•	• ocean

On the back of this sheet, draw a mammal that you have seen today. Write two sentences about it.

Brain Builder

Name _____

What do you know about caring for pets?

Words to Know

mammal   shelter

exercise

A Perfect Pet

Many people have mammals for pets. A dog is one kind of mammal that can be a good pet. Dogs come in all sizes. Some dogs need a lot of room for exercise. Some need just a little. People need to choose dogs that are right for them.

All dogs need love and care. A puppy needs to eat a few times each day. An older dog might need to eat just once each day. All dogs need water and shelter. Taking care of a dog can be a lot of work. It can be a lot of fun, too!

1. **Think** about the passage. Why should people choose dogs that are right for them?

_____
_____
_____

2. **Read** the words below. **Circle** the words that tell what all dogs need. (*Hint: There are four of them.*)

water   blanket   food

love   shelter   collar

3. What would be another good title for this passage? Why?

_____
_____
_____

Brain Builder

On the back of this sheet, draw a picture of a dog and its owner. Show each thing that the dog needs. Write two sentences about your picture.

13

Where do mammals live?

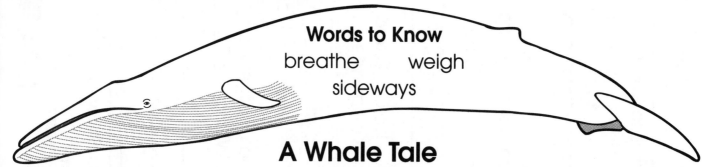

Words to Know

breathe   weigh

sideways

A Whale Tale

A whale lives in the ocean. It looks a lot like a fish, but it is not. A whale is a mammal.

Fish have up and down tail fins. Whales have sideways tail fins. Fish breathe with gills. Whales go to the top of the water to breathe. A baby fish comes from an egg. A baby whale is born alive.

Some whales are the same size as a large dog. Some whales are a lot bigger. A blue whale is the biggest mammal. Its tongue might weigh as much as an elephant. A baby blue whale is as big as a bus!

1. **Look** back in the passage.
   a. **Underline** the word that means almost the same as "sea".
   b. **Circle** the word that means the same as "big."

2. **Read** the words below. **Write** "fish" or "whale."

   mammal _____   sideways fins _____

   gills _____   egg _____

3. Whales are mammals. Why might some people think they are fish? _____

   _____

   _____

On the back of this sheet, write two ways that whales and fish are the same. Write two ways that they are not the same.

Brain Builder

What is an insect?

Going Buggy

Insects come in many shapes. They come in a lot of colors and sizes, too. Most insects have wings. Others do not. Some insects have five eyes. Some have no eyes at all!

All insects have three body parts and six legs. Some insects do not taste with their mouths. They taste with their feet! An insect does not smell with a nose. It smells with feelers. Most insects do not have ears. They hear with small hairs on their bodies. Insects are special animals!

1. **Look** back in the passage. **Underline** the sentence that tells how insects hear.

2. **Read** each set of sentences below. **Write** "yes" or "no."

   a. A spider has eight legs. Is a spider an insect? _____
   b. A butterfly has six legs. Is a butterfly an insect? _____
   c. An ant has three body parts. Is an ant an insect? _____

3. Why do you think the author calls insects special?

   _____

   _____

Brain Builder

On the back of this sheet, draw a new kind of insect. Write two sentences that tell why it is an insect.

Name _____

Where do butterflies come from?

Insect Changes

Some insects change a lot when they grow. A butterfly starts as an egg. The egg is small. It might be as small as the top of a pin. A caterpillar hatches from the egg. It eats a lot. It grows and grows. One day the caterpillar makes a house. The house is like a hard shell. It is called a chrysalis. The house is very still for a long time. Then it cracks. A butterfly comes out. Once the insect was an egg. Now it is a butterfly!

Words to Know
change
caterpillar
chrysalis

1. **Look** back in the passage. **Underline** the sentences that tell about the size of a butterfly egg.

2. **Read** each word. **Draw** a line to the word that is almost the same.

   starts •   • opens
   still   •   • begins
   cracks •   • quiet

3. **Think** about the passage. **Number** the words in order.

   a. ____ caterpillar
   b. ____ egg
   c. ____ butterfly
   d. ____ chrysalis

On the back of this sheet, draw four pictures to show how an egg changes into a butterfly. Make the pictures look like a comic strip.

Brain Builder

What do you know about ants?

Words to Know
job   queens   workers

Do you know that
every ant has a job?
Some ants are queens. Their
job is to lay eggs. Other ants are
workers. Some workers make
homes called anthills or look for
food. Some workers take care
of the queens. Others take care
of the baby ants. Worker
ants have a lot to do!

1. **Write** the words for two kinds of ants that have jobs.

   _____   _____

2. What kind of ant finds food? _____

3. How many jobs does a queen ant do? _____

4. **Circle** the word in the passage that tells where ants live.

5. What is a good title for this passage? Why? _____

   _____

   _____

Brain Builder

How are ants like people? How are they different?
Write your ideas on the back of this sheet.

INSECTS: *Ant behavior* 17

How are reptiles different from amphibians?

Words to Know
moist   smooth
scales

Can you tell reptiles from amphibians? These tips might help! Amphibians have smooth skin. The skin is moist. Reptiles have dry skin. Most of them have scales, too. Amphibian eggs do not have shells. They feel like jelly. Reptile eggshells can be hard or soft. Most amphibian babies do not look like their parents. Baby reptiles do. Look closely, and you can tell reptiles from amphibians!

1. **Write** the words below in the correct columns.

scales	dry skin	smooth
moist skin	eggs like jelly	look like their parents

reptiles   **amphibians**

_____   _____

_____   _____

_____   _____

2. **Look** in the passage. **Circle** two words that tell you how reptile eggs might feel.

3. **Read** each clue. **Write** whether the animal is a reptile or an amphibian.
    a. A turtle has a shell made of scales. _____
    b. A toad lays eggs that do not have shells. _____

What is a good title for this passage? Why? Write your ideas on the back of this sheet.

Brain Builder

Name _____

How can you tell a frog from a toad?

Words to Know
blink   dull
chew

Learn About Frogs and Toads!

Frogs and toads are amphibians. They are a lot alike. Frogs and toads do not have tails. They do not chew their food. They blink their eyes to push their food down. Frogs and toads are different in some ways, too.

Frogs have smooth, wet skin. Some of them are colorful. Most frogs have long back legs. They can jump well. Frogs live in or by the water. A frog has teeth in its top jaw.

Toads have bumpy, dry skin. Many toads are dull brown or gray. Toads have short back legs. They walk or hop. Most toads live on land. Toads do not have teeth.

1. **Think** about the passage. **Write** one way frogs and toads are alike.

   _____

2. **Look** back at the passage. **Complete** each sentence.

   a. Frogs and toads do not _____ their food.

   b. Most frogs have _____ back legs.

   c. Most toads live on _____.

3. Why do you think most frogs can jump better than toads?

   _____

Brain Builder

Do you think frogs and toads are more alike or more different? Write your ideas on the back of this sheet.

Name_____

What do you know about snakes?

Words to Know

poison   fangs
swallow

Snakes

What has no legs, but can move very fast? A snake! Snakes are reptiles. They have small teeth. Snakes do not use their teeth to chew. They swallow their food whole. They can eat animals that are bigger than their mouths!

Some snakes have fangs. The fangs have poison. Most snakes do not have fangs, though. Most snakes do not harm us. Some snakes can be pets, but it is a good idea to stay away from strange snakes.

1. **Circle** yes or no.
   a. All snakes have fangs.   yes   no
   b. Most snakes harm people.   yes   no
   c. A snake swallows its food in one piece.   yes   no

2. How can you tell if a snake has poison? _____
   _____

3. **Think** about the passage. **Complete** each sentence.
   a. Snakes do not have _____.
   b. Snakes _____ their food whole.

4. **Circle** the word in the passage that means almost the same as "hurt."

5. **Underline** the word in the passage that means almost the same as "all in one piece."

Snakes do not use their teeth to chew. What do you think they use them for? Write your ideas on the back of this sheet.

Brain Builder

PTILES/AMPHIBIANS: *Snakes*

Why is it important to know what the weather is?

What Is the Weather Today?

Would you wear flip-flops in the snow? Of course not! It would be too cold for flip-flops. The weather helps you know what kind of clothes to wear.

The weather helps you make plans, too. When it rains, you may plan to take an umbrella. When it is sunny, you may plan to work in a garden. When it is windy and warm, you may plan to fly a kite. When it is calm, you may plan to take a boat ride. It helps to know what the weather is!

Words to Know
garden
plan
windy

1. What are some kinds of weather? **Underline** four words in the passage that tell you.

2. Why might calm weather make some people happy?

   _____

   _____

3. **Read** each list of words below. **Draw** a line through the word in each list that is not a weather word.

sleet	boat	snow	rain
sunny	cold	flip-flops	work
garden	windy	hot	warm

Brain Builder

Why should you know what the weather is before you get ready for school? Write your thoughts on the back of this sheet.

Why might someone watch the weather?

Words to Know
station
satellite
cloud

Weather Watching

Weather watchers find out about the weather in a lot of ways.

Some weather watchers work at weather stations. They keep an eye on the air and wind.

Some weather watchers use balloons. They send weather balloons into the air. The balloons show what the air and wind are doing.

Other weather watchers look at pictures sent by satellite. The pictures show where clouds and storms are.

Look at the weather chart below. **Use** it to answer the questions.

Weather

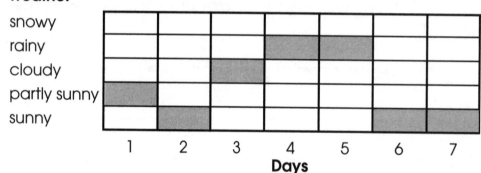

1. What kinds of weather were there during the seven days?

_____

2. What kind of weather showed up most often?_____

3. Do you think day 3 was a good day for a picnic? Why or why not?

_____

Why is a weather watcher's job important? Write your thoughts on the back of this sheet.

Brain Builder

What do you know about storms?

Stormy Weather

Sometimes they move slowly. Sometimes they move fast. Flash! Boom! Storms are weather that goes wild. Thunderstorms, tornadoes, and hurricanes are three kinds of storms.

Thunderstorms have rain, lightning, and thunder. Sometimes they have wind, too.

Tornadoes are clouds that spin and roar. They have winds that blow very hard. Rain may fall. Lightning may strike. Thunder may boom.

Hurricanes are large storms. They grow over the oceans. Then they hit land. Tornadoes and thunderstorms may come with hurricanes. Watch out for these storms, and learn what to do if you are in one.

Look the chart below. **Think** about the passage. **Draw** a **+** in each box that tells about the matching storm.

	rain	thunder	lightning	wind	spinning cloud	grows over an ocean
thunderstorm						
tornado						
hurricane						

Brain Builder

Read the chart. What kind of storm is the wildest? Why? Write your ideas on the back of this sheet.

Name_____

What makes day and night?

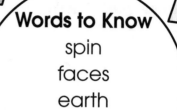

Words to Know
spin
faces
earth

It is early morning. You watch the sun rise. You feel the warm sunshine. The night ends. A new day begins. Why does this happen?

Think about a time you were outside spinning. You went very fast and got dizzy. Our earth spins, too. You cannot feel it spin. It takes 24 hours for the earth to spin around one time. That is one day. When the side of the earth you live on faces the sun, you have day. When it faces away from the sun, you have night. Some people are having day right now. Other people are having night. The earth spins to make day and night.

1. **Read** each sentence below.
   Circle it if it tells about something you do when your side of the earth faces the sun.
   Underline it if it tells about something you do when your side of the earth faces away from the sun.

   a. You are eating lunch.   c. You are watching for shooting stars.

   b. You are sleeping.   d. You are leaving school in the afternoon.

2. **Look** back in the passage. **Underline** the sentence that tells why we do not get dizzy as the earth spins.

3. What is a good title for this passage? Why? _____

_____

On the back of this sheet, draw a picture of what you might do when your side of the earth faces away from the sun.

Brain Builder

24 SOLAR SYSTEM: *Earth's day & night*

Name _____ *Details, main idea*

What do you know about the moon?

By the Light of the Moon

Walk at night when the moon is full. The moon shines on you. The moon is bright but does not give off its own light. It gives off sunlight. Sunlight shines on the moon and bounces off.

One night you see a lot of the moon. It is full and bright. On another night, you do not see much of the moon. It is a slice of light. Is the moon changing shapes? No, it stays the same shape. It is dark where the sun does not shine on the moon. From the earth, we see the light on the moon. We do not see the dark part of the moon.

1. **Think** about the passage. **Read** each sentence below. **Draw** a + in the box if the sentence is true.

    ☐ a. Sunlight bounces off the moon.
    ☐ b. The moon starts off big, then gets smaller and smaller.
    ☐ c. The sun shines on all of the moon all of the time.

2. **Read** each sentence below. **Find** the word that belongs in the sentence. **Write** its number on the line.

    1. dark   2. shape   3. sunlight   4. moon

    a. We see _____ on the moon.
    b. The moon does not change its _____ .
    c. The _____ looks like a big ball.
    d. Part of the moon can be _____ and the other part light.

Brain Builder

A long time ago, some people thought that the moon died every month and then grew back. What would you tell those people about the moon? Write your thoughts on the back of this sheet.

Why is the sun important to us?

Words to Know
life
closest
million

Our Sunny Star

What star is most important to us? The sun is! It gives us heat. It gives us light. If there were no heat or light, there would be no life on the earth. Plants need sunlight to make their own food. People and animals eat plants.

The sun is the earth's closest star. It is about 93 million miles away from the earth. It looks as if it is the largest star, but it is not. Many other stars are bigger.

Where the sun is in the sky is important to us. The North Pole and the South Pole are very cold. They do not get much sunshine. Other places on the earth get very hot. The sun shines down on them.

1. **Look** back in the passage. **Circle** the words that tell two things the sun gives us.

2. Why does the sun look as if it is the largest star? _____

   _____

3. What would happen if there were no sun? _____

   _____

4. **Read** each group of words. **Circle** the word that does not belong.

   a. star   light   b. people   animals   c. car   sun
      heat   miles   hot   plants   star   earth

On the back of this sheet, write a new title for the passage. Write why you think it is a good title.

Brain Builder

©2000 The Education Center, Inc. • Comprehension Connections • TEC4112 • Key p. 63

Name _____

Why is it important to be healthy?

Words to Know
exercise
germs
healthy

A Healthy Body

What does your body need to be healthy? It needs good foods like apples, bread, and milk. They help you grow and stay strong. Your body needs to be kept clean. Baths help get rid of germs. Germs can make you sick. Your body needs plenty of sleep each night. It needs exercise, too. Exercise is good for your heart. Running and bike riding help keep you fit. It feels good to be healthy!

1. What is the passage mostly about? _____

_____

2. **Look** back in the passage. What is one way to keep your body healthy? _____

3. **Use** the words below to complete the sentences.

healthy   germs   exercise   heart

a. Taking a bath cleans away _____.

b. Running and bike riding are _____.

c. If you do not sleep enough, you may not stay _____.

d. Swimming is good for your _____.

Brain Builder

On the back of this sheet, draw a picture of yourself doing your favorite kind of exercise. Write why it is good for you.

What do you know about making good food choices?

Words to Know
vegetables
dairy   energy

Good Food Choices

We need energy for all the things we do.
We need it to run, play, or read. You are using
energy right now! We get energy when we eat
the right foods. Some foods help us grow, too.
Breads, vegetables, and fruits are good for us.
Meats, beans, and dairy foods are also good.
Foods like cake and chips are not as good
for us. They have a lot of sugar or fat.
Be sure to pick the best foods
for your body!

1. **Read** the words below. **Circle** the four foods that are best for you.

   fruits   meats   candy   beans   cheese   cake

2. **Look** back in the passage. **Complete** the sentences.

   a. It takes _____ to read a book.

   b. People should not eat a lot of _____ or sugar.

   c. _____ gives people energy and helps them grow.

3. **Circle** yes or no.

   a. People need energy to jog.   yes   no

   b. Boys and girls need energy to color pictures.   yes   no

   c. People get a lot of good energy from cookies.   yes   no

What might happen if you do not eat enough vegetables or
fruit? Write your ideas on the back of this sheet.

Brain Builder

Why is it important to keep your teeth healthy?

Words to Know
dentist
cavities   floss

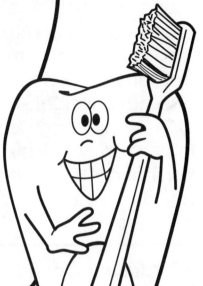

Super Smiles

Do you know that you have about 20 teeth? It is a big job to keep them all healthy! To keep them healthy, eat foods like milk and cheese. Do not eat a lot of sugar. It can make holes in your teeth called cavities. If a cavity gets too big, the tooth it is in will hurt.

Brush your teeth after each meal. Brushing gets food and germs off your teeth. Use floss each day to clean between your teeth. Try to visit a dentist one or two times a year. Smile if you want healthy teeth!

1. **Read** the words. **Draw** an **X** on each food that is not good for your teeth. *(Hint: There are four of them.)*

    candy   cheese   cake   cookies   milk   soda

2. **Think** about the underlined words below. **Rewrite** each sentence to make it true.
   a. Cavities are <u>bumps on</u> your teeth.

   _____

   b. <u>Sugar</u> makes teeth healthy.

   _____

3. **Look** back in the passage. **Underline** the sentence that tells you why you should brush your teeth.

Brain Builder

Think about the passage. On the back of this sheet, make a poster that shows three ways to care for your teeth.

What does it mean to take up space?

Matter Everywhere!

Look high. Look low. Matter is every place you look! All things are made of matter. Bikes and milk are matter. The air inside a balloon is matter, too. These things are the same in two ways. They all take up space and have weight.

There are many kinds of matter. Matter can look, smell, feel, taste, or sound different. It can be shiny or dull. It can be big or small. It can even be something that you cannot see at all!

Words to Know
air
weight
dull

1. **Circle** yes or no.

   a. Matter takes up space.   yes   no
   b. A desk is made of matter.   yes   no
   c. You can see all matter.   yes   no
   d. Some matter is wet.   yes   no
   e. All matter is very heavy.   yes   no

2. **Look** back in the passage. **Circle** the word that tells how heavy something is.

3. **Look** back in the passage. **Underline** the word that means "not bright."

4. **Write** in your own words what "matter" means. _____

   _____

   _____

   Look around the room. On the back of this sheet, draw three things you see that are matter. Write how you know they are matter.

   Brain Builder

Name _____

What do you know about matter?

Words to Know
shape
liquid
gas

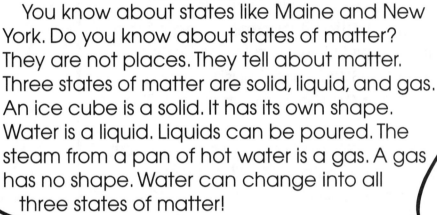

You know about states like Maine and New York. Do you know about states of matter? They are not places. They tell about matter. Three states of matter are solid, liquid, and gas. An ice cube is a solid. It has its own shape. Water is a liquid. Liquids can be poured. The steam from a pan of hot water is a gas. A gas has no shape. Water can change into all three states of matter!

1. How are a solid and a gas the same? _____

   _____

2. How are a solid and a gas different? _____

   _____

3. **Draw** a line from each word on the left to the matching group of words.

   a. liquid •   • has no shape
   b. solid   •   • can be poured
   c. gas   •   • has its own shape

4. **List** the three states of matter. _____

Brain Builder

What is a good title for this passage? Why? Write your ideas on the back of this sheet.

Name_____

Why do some things float?

Words to Know
matter
sink
weighs

Sink or Float?

Rocks are made of matter. Ships are, too. A lot of things tell about matter. One thing is if it sinks or floats. When something is put in water, it pushes some of the water away. Some things push away a lot of water. Some things push away a little. If they push away enough water, they float. If they do not, they sink like rocks.

It can be hard to guess if something will sink or float. A ship is big. It weighs a lot. A ship looks like it cannot stay on top of water, but it does!

1. **Look** back in the passage.

   a. **Write** the word that means "stay on top." _____

   b. **Write** the word that means "go to the bottom." _____

   c. **Write** the word that means the opposite of "pull." _____

2. **Write** "sink" or "float."
   a. Rocks _____ in water.

   b. Boats _____ in water.

3. Some things float because _____

   _____

What is the best way to tell if something can float in water? Why? Write your ideas on the back of this sheet.

Brain Builder

Name _____

What are some different kinds of homes?

Home, Sweet Home

There is no place like home! Some homes are big. Some are small. Some homes have a lot of rooms. Some have just a few. Homes are different all over the world.

Some people live where there are a lot of trees. They may have homes made of wood. Some people live where it snows a lot. Their homes may have strong, pointy roofs. The snow slides off this kind of roof. Some people live where the land is very wet. Their homes may be made on stilts. The stilts keep their homes high and dry. Homes near and far are special places!

1. **Draw** a line to match each word with the group of words that means almost the same thing.

    a. home •   • not the same
    b. different •   • not many
    c. few •   • place to live
    d. dry •   • not wet

2. **Look** back in the passage. **Underline** the sentence that tells why homes in wet places may be on stilts.

3. **Read** the sentences below. **Underline** the one that best tells what the passage is mostly about.

    a. It rains a lot in some places.

    b. There are many different kinds of homes.

    c. It is fun to live where it snows a lot.

Brain Builder

Think about the homes where it snows a lot. Why do you think they have strong roofs? Write your ideas on the back of this sheet.

©2000 The Education Center, Inc. • Comprehension Connections • TEC4112 • Key p. 63

Where does food come from?

Words to Know
healthy
cool
countries

What Is for Lunch?

It is time to eat! All people need to eat good foods to be healthy. People do not eat the same foods, though.

Rice grows in places that are very wet. People who live there may eat a lot of rice. Fruits grow in places that are hot. People who live there may eat many fruits. Potatoes do not grow well where it is hot. They grow better in places that are cool. People who live in cool places may eat a lot of potatoes.

Some people sell the food they grow to people in other countries. No matter where you live, there are great foods!

1. **Look** back in the passage. **Write** the food that grows best in each kind of place below.
   a. hot   _____
   b. wet   _____
   c. cool   _____

2. **Look** back in the passage. **Follow** the directions below.
   a. **Use** a red crayon to underline the sentence that tells where fruits grow well.
   b. **Use** a blue crayon to underline the sentence that tells where rice grows well.

3. What is this passage mostly about? _____

   _____

Think about the passage. If you want to grow plants for food, what should you think about first? Write your ideas on the back of this sheet.

Brain Builder

What can children do outside for fun?

Words to Know
icy
forest
mountains

Children all over the world have fun outside. The places they live help them know what they can do outside. Some boys and girls live where there are a lot of icy lakes. They can play ice hockey. Some children live where it is warm all year. They can play a lot of games, but not ice hockey! They might play soccer instead. Some boys and girls live near a forest or the mountains. They can camp in tents. Some other children live in cities. They can go to a park. There are fun things to do everywhere you go!

1. **Complete** each sentence below with a sport from the passage.
   a. Canada is a very cold country. It is a good place to play

   _____.

   b. Mexico is a warm country. It is a good place to play

   _____.

2. **Circle** the word in the passage that means the same as "woods."

3. **Think** about the passage. Why do children from different places sometimes do different things outside?

   _____

   _____

Brain Builder

What is a good title for this passage? Why? Write your ideas on the back of this sheet.

Name_____

What do you know about pioneer schools?

Words to Know
share
slates
chalkboards

Schools Past and Present

Long ago, most schools had just one room. There was only one teacher. Children of all ages learned together. The schools had few books. The boys and girls had to bring books from home. They had to share the books. There was not much paper. The children had to write on small chalkboards called slates.

Today most schools have a lot of rooms. Most of the time, boys and girls who are about the same age share a teacher and a room. The schools have many books. The children use paper, pencils, and crayons. Some of them even use computers!

1. **Look** back in the passage.

    a. **Underline** the sentence that tells why students had to share books.

    b. **Circle** the word that tells what children wrote on long ago.

2. Most students today do not use slates. **Write** a word from the passage on each line below to tell what they might use to do their work.

    _____   _____   _____

3. **Think** about the passage. **Write** one way that schools from long ago and schools of today are different. _____

    _____

Do you think it would have been easier or harder to be a teacher long ago? Why? Write your ideas on the back of this sheet.

Brain Builder

Name _____

What does it mean to travel?

Words to Know
pioneers   oxen   flatboat

Pioneer Trips

How did pioneers go on trips? Sometimes they walked. Sometimes they went in wagons. Some wagons were pulled by horses. Some were pulled by mules or oxen.

To go on a river, pioneers rode flatboats. There was room for a family on a flatboat. There was room for its animals. There was even room for its wagon!

Now people take trips in a lot of ways. They ride in cars and trains. They ride in trucks and planes, too. In one hour, a car can go as far as a wagon could in about one week. Trips can be a lot faster now!

1. **Look** back in the passage. **Underline** three kinds of animals that the pioneers used for trips.

2. **Write** one way to travel that is <u>not</u> in the passage. _____

   _____

3. **Read** the words below. **Circle** each one that names a way pioneers did <u>not</u> travel. *(Hint: There are three of them.)*

   plane   horse   wagon   oxen   bus   car

4. Why was travel slow for pioneers? _____

   _____

Brain Builder

On the back of this sheet, list the ways that you and your friends go to school.

How did pioneer children help at home?

Work and Play

Pioneer homes were not like homes today. They did not have sinks with running water. They did not have a way to keep food cold. The children did chores to help at home. Some children had to carry water from a river. Some of them cooked and sewed. Some of them planted crops or milked the cows.

The boys and girls played sometimes, too. They made most of their toys. They used sticks to make whistles. They used string to make balls. They used rocks, sticks, and leaves to make forts. Pioneer children worked and played hard. They must have slept well at night!

1. **Circle** the word in the passage that means the same as "jobs."

2. **Look** back in the passage. **Write** two chores that pioneer children could do inside. _____   _____

3. **Look** back in the passage. **Write** two things that pioneer children used to play with. _____   _____

4. Why do you think pioneers had to carry water? _____

_____

_____

Why does the author think that pioneer children must have slept well at night? Write your ideas on the back of this sheet.

Brain Builder

What do you know about cities and towns?

Words to Know
community   buildings   fewer

Large and Small

I see a lot of people. I see a lot of cars and buses. I see a lot of tall buildings. I am in a city. A city is a large community. A lot of people do not know each other. There are a lot of schools and stores in a city. There are parks and movie theaters.

I see fewer people. I see fewer cars and buses. I see fewer buildings. Now I am in a town. A town is a small community. A lot of people know each other in a town. Sometimes they get together to have fun.

1. **Read** each sentence below. **Underline** the one that is the main idea of the passage.

   a. A city and a town have buildings.
   b. A city is a large community and a town is a small one.
   c. There are sidewalks in a city.

2. **Think** about the passage. **Read** the words below. **Draw** an **X** in the box beside each group of words that tells about a city.

   ☐ a lot of tall buildings   ☐ a large community
   ☐ not many people   ☐ lots of open land
   ☐ a lot of cars and buses   ☐ a lot of stores

3. Would a town have as many stores and schools as a city? Why or why not? _____

   _____

Brain Builder

On the back of this sheet, write about your community. Be sure to tell if it is a city or a town.

What helps people in your community decide how to spend time outside?

Outdoors Fun

Do you live near the mountains? Do you live near an ocean? Where you live helps you choose what to do outdoors.

Some people live by the ocean. There are a lot of things for them to do outdoors. They might swim. They might jump the waves. They might play in the sand.

Some people live near the mountains. There are a lot of things for them to do outdoors, too. They might hike. They might go rock climbing. They might go skiing if there is snow. There are fun things to do outdoors no matter where you live!

Words to Know
outdoors
mountains
ocean

1. **Read** each word or group of words below. **Write** it in the correct column.

   hike   jump the waves   snow-ski

   swim   write in the sand   climb rocks

   Mountains   **Ocean**

   _____   _____

   _____   _____

   _____   _____

2. **Think** about the passage. Why can't all people go rock climbing?

   _____

3. If you lived on a farm, what might you do outdoors for fun?

   _____

   What can a person in your community do outdoors for fun? On the back of this sheet, draw a picture to show one of your ideas.

   Brain Builder

Name_____

When might you need to use a map?

Going Places With Maps

Maps are fun to use! Some people use maps to find places. Some people use maps to find out how far away a place is. Some people use maps to plan trips. Every map has a key. A map key tells what the pictures on the map mean.

Help Sam find his way around Camp Lots-of-Fun. Use the map and directions below.

Key
-  = cabin
- = forest
- = lake
- = mountains
- = dining hall

Camp Lots-of-Fun

1. **Read** each sentence below. **Draw** a line on the map to show the way Sam goes.

   a. Sam leaves the cabin to swim in the lake.
   b. Sam goes to walk in the mountains.
   c. Sam goes to the dining hall for lunch.
   d. Sam goes for a boat ride.
   e. Sam goes to the forest to look for birds.

2. **Draw** a line from the beginning of the sentence to its ending.
   a. The map helps Sam •   • has a key.
   b. Every map •   • find places.
   c. A key tells us •   • trips.
   d. People can use maps to plan •   • about the map pictures.

Brain Builder

Why do you think maps need keys? Write your thoughts on the back of this sheet.

What things do all people need?

Living on an Island

Make believe you and a friend are alone on an island. What do you need to stay alive? Three things all people need are food, clothing, and shelter. Food helps you grow and work. Clothing helps keep you safe when the weather is bad. Shelter does, too. There are many kinds of shelters. Homes, cars, and tents are shelters.

Now think about your wants. Wants are things you would like to have but can live without. What would you want to have on the island? You may want a bike. Your friend may want books. People have different wants. People have the same needs.

Words to Know
alive   clothing
shelter

---

1. **Read** the words below. **Circle** the three things that are needs.

toys	cars	shelter	bed
food	dogs	clothing	plate

2. **Underline** the sentence in the passage that tells what wants are.

3. **Read** each sentence below. **Circle** yes if the sentence is true. **Circle** no if the sentence is not true.

   a. All people have the same wants.   yes   no
   b. All people have the same needs.   yes   no
   c. A school is a shelter.   yes   no
   d. All people need a bed.   yes   no

Make believe you are on the island in the passage. On the back of this sheet, draw and label three things you would need. Then draw and label three things you would want.

Brain Builder

Name _____

What are some things people buy?

Words to Know
goods
services
pay

DELIVERY PERSON

What Are You Buying?

Sue buys skates. Joe buys ice cream. Pat buys a book. Skates, ice cream, and books are goods. Goods are things that people make and then sell. You can see and touch goods.

Sue pays the doctor to give her a checkup. Joe pays to get his hair cut. Pat pays for a taxi ride. The checkup, haircut, and taxi ride are services. A service is a job that someone is paid to do. A lot of people are paid for their services. Some of them are teachers, firefighters, and nurses.

1. **Find** the sentence in the passage that tells what goods are. **Underline** it with a blue crayon.

2. **Find** the sentence in the passage that tells what a service is. **Underline** it with a red crayon.

3. **Read** each sentence below. **Circle** yes or no.

   a. All things you buy are called services.   yes   no
   b. Shoes and socks are goods.   yes   no
   c. A police officer does a service for people.   yes   no

4. **Read** the words below. **Circle** the services. **Underline** the goods.

   teaching   driving a bus   cars   flowers   fixing cars

Brain Builder

On the back of this sheet, draw and label a picture of a good. Then draw and label a picture of someone doing a service.

What happens when stores do not have enough of the toys that children want?

ON AIR

Words to Know

supply   demand   cost

There is a hot new toy in town! It is the Trat! It is a trick bat. All the stores have sold out of Trats. A Trat cost $5.00 when it came out. Now it costs $50.00! Children are going batty over Trats!

A lot of people want to buy Trats. This means there is a big demand for them. There are too few Trats. This means the supply is low. There is a big demand but not enough supply. That can make the cost go up.

1. **Read** each sentence below.
   Draw a **+** beside each one that tells what might happen if stores do not have enough of the toys that children want.
   _____ The cost will go up.
   _____ The toy will get lost.
   _____ The toy will be hard to find.

2. **Read** the sentences below. **Write** each word in the correct blank.

   supply   demand   cost

   All the people I know want new toy cars. The _____ is high.
   There are enough new toy cars for everyone who wants one.
   The stores have a big _____ of them. The _____
      of the new toy car is $5.00.

   On the back of this sheet, draw a picture of what might happen if a store has more demand than supply.

   Brain Builder

Name _____

What does it mean to be a citizen?

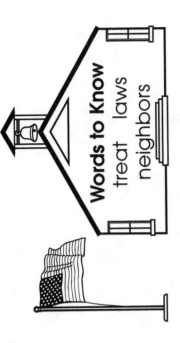

Words to Know

treat   laws

neighbors

Good Citizens

Ann <u>shares</u> her crayons. Tim listens to the teacher. Jill and Bob take turns. Ann, Tim, Jill, and Bob follow the rules. They treat the things in their classroom well. They are all good class citizens. A citizen is a person who <u>belongs to</u> a group of people. These students are citizens of a class. They are citizens of a town, too. They help make the town a nice place to be. They do not <u>litter</u>. They help keep the town clean. They follow the laws. Good citizens can be great friends and neighbors!

1. **Look** back in the passage. **Circle** the word that means "people who live near each other."

2. **Look** at the underlined words in the passage. **Write** each one on the correct line below.

   a. is part of _____

   b. lets other people use _____

   c. drop trash on the ground _____

3. **Draw** an **X** in the box beside each group of words that tells about a good class citizen.

   ☐ a. follows the rules

   ☐ b. cares for just himself

   ☐ c. takes good care of his math book

Brain Builder

What might happen if students are not good class citizens? Write your ideas on the back of this sheet.

45

What does it mean to be responsible?

Words to Know
citizens
respect
rights

Class Citizens

You can count on good class citizens! They take care of their responsibilities. This means they do the things they need to do. Good class citizens follow the rules. They show respect. They listen to the teacher. They listen to each other. They help keep the classroom clean.

When students do these things, they respect the rights of other students. All students have the right to learn. They have the right to be safe. They have the right to be treated fairly, too. Rights and responsibilities help make classrooms nice places to be!

1. **Read** each sentence below. **Draw** a **+** beside each one that tells about a good class citizen.

   a. Jane raises her hand for a turn.
   b. Kelly talks when James is reading to the class.
   c. Will helps Sally put the books away.

2. **Complete** each sentence with a word below. *(Hint: You will not use one of the words.)*

citizens	need	respect	right

   a. Responsibilities are things people _____ to do.
   b. The students have a _____ to be safe in school.
   c. Students are _____ of a class.

Do you think it is important for students to have responsibilities? Why or why not? Write your ideas on the back of this sheet.

Brain Builder

Name _____

Words to Know

law
obey
community

Why do we need rules?

Kate needs to do her math work. Then she can watch TV. That is a rule in her home.

Sam walks in the hall at school. It is against the rules to run. It would not be safe.

Mr. Brown drives his car. He stops the car at the stop sign. He follows the law.

Good citizens follow the rules at home and at school. They obey the laws in their communities. Rules and laws help people know what to do. They help keep people safe. They help make things fair, too. It is a good idea to obey rules and laws!

1. **Think** about the passage. **Read** the words below. **Write** each one on the correct line.

| community   home   safe   follow |

a. obey   _____
b. house   _____
c. city or town _____
d. not hurt   _____

2. **Think** about the passage. What might happen if Kate does not follow the rule about watching TV? _____
_____

3. What is a good title for this passage? Why? _____
_____

Brain Builder

How do rules and laws help keep people safe? Write your ideas on the back of this sheet.

CIVICS & GOVERNMENT: *Rules & laws*

47

Name _____

What do you know about the White House?

Words to Know

office   visits
president

A Special House

The president of the United States lives and works in a very big house. It is called the White House. It has three <u>stories</u>. It has more than 100 rooms. Some rooms are for visits. One of them is called the Blue Room. Some rooms are for the president's family. One of them is a kitchen. One of them has a place to bowl! A lot of rooms are for work. The president works in a room called the Oval Office. There is no other house just like the White House. It is a very special place!

1. **Read** the underlined word above. **Think** about what it means in the passage. **Circle** the word below that is almost the same.

   books   floors   window

2. How many rooms does the White House have? **Circle** the answer below.

   100   more than 75   less than 90

3. **Look** back in the passage. **Circle** the word that tells what the president's family might do for fun.

4. Why do you think the room where the president works is called the Oval Office?

   _____

   _____

Think about the passage. Would you like to live in the White House? Why or why not? Write your answer on the back of this sheet.

Brain Builder

Name_____

What are some ways to celebrate birthdays?

Words to Know
fourth   parade
fireworks

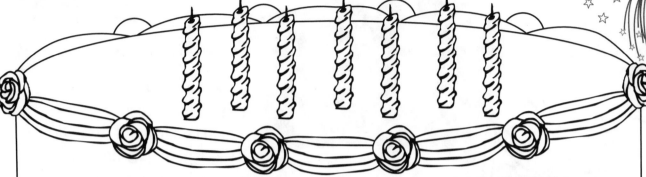

Do you know that the United States has a birthday? It is on July 4. The Fourth of July is a time to show love for the United States. It is a time to have fun. People have fun in a lot of ways on this day. Some people play music. Some people watch parades or have picnics. They might play games, too. Some towns have red, white, and blue fireworks. Bang! Boom! Happy birthday, America!

1. What is a good title for the passage?_____
   _____

2. **Look** back in the passage. **Write** the word that is another name for the United States. _____

3. When is America's birthday? _____

4. **Read** the sentences below. **Draw** an **X** beside the one that is not true.
   a. The Fourth of July is a fun day for a lot of people.
   b. Many people play in the snow on the Fourth of July.
   c. People play music on the Fourth of July.

Brain Builder

Look at your answer for number 1. On the back of this sheet, write why you think it is a good title.

Name_____

What are some things that stand for the United States?

Words to Know
state   stripe
row

Flag Facts

What is red, white, and blue and stands for the United States? The flag! The first U.S. flag had six white stripes and seven red stripes. There was a stripe for each of the first 13 states. There was a star for each state, too. The stars were in a circle or in rows. Now the flag has 13 stripes and 50 stars. There is a star for every state. The stars are in rows. Hooray for the Red, White, and Blue!

1. **Write** "yes" or "no."

   a. The first U.S. flag had 13 stripes. _____

   b. The first flag had more stars than today's flag. _____

   c. The U.S. flag has always looked the same. _____

2. Why are there 50 stars on the flag? _____

   _____

3. Some people call the U.S. flag "The Stars and Stripes." Do you think this is a good name for the flag? Why or why not? _____

   _____

Think about the passage. How is the flag we have today like the first U.S. flag? How is it different? Write your ideas on the back of this sheet.

Brain Builder

What does it mean to be free?

Words to Know
leader   slavery
announce

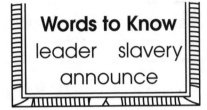

A Good Leader

Do you know who is on the penny? Abraham Lincoln is! He was the 16th president of the United States. He gave good speeches. He was kind and smart.

Long ago when Lincoln lived, black people were sold as slaves. They had no rights. They had to work hard for other people.

Lincoln knew that slavery was wrong. He worked to stop it. He announced that slaves would be free. They would own land. They would work for money. A few years later, slavery stopped. Lincoln helped make the United States a better place!

1. **Circle** the words that tell about Abraham Lincoln. *(Hint: There are four words.)*

    kind   president   shy   smart   mean   slave   speaker

2. **Circle** yes or no.
    a. Lincoln announced that slavery would stop.   yes   no
    b. The first U.S. president was Abraham Lincoln.   yes   no
    c. Lincoln was too shy to speak to crowds.   yes   no
    d. Lincoln did not believe in slavery.   yes   no

3. Why do you think the author titled this passage "A Good Leader"?

    _____

    _____

Brain Builder

If Abraham Lincoln were alive today, what would you want to tell him? Why? Write your ideas on the back of this sheet.

Name _____

What do you know about laws?

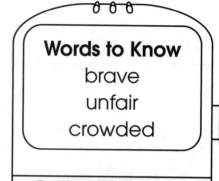

Words to Know
brave
unfair
crowded

A Bus Ride

Rosa Parks was brave. Her bravery helped change an unfair law. A long time ago, black people had to sit at the back of the bus. If a bus was crowded, they had to give their seats to white people.

One day Rosa was riding the bus. There were no more seats for white people. Rosa was told to stand. She would not. The police took Rosa to jail. Then black people stopped riding the bus. They would not ride the bus until the law changed. Rosa had helped them be brave, too. Now black people can sit in any seat on the bus. Thank you, Rosa Parks!

1. **Look** back in the passage. **Circle** the word that tells the kind of law that Rosa Parks helped change.

2. Why did Rosa Parks go to jail? _____
   _____

3. **Number** the sentences below in the order they happened:
   ___ The police took Rosa to jail.
   ___ Rosa would not give up her seat.
   ___ Rosa had helped change the law.
   ___ Black people stopped riding the bus.

What do you think the author wants you to know about Rosa Parks? Write your ideas on the back of this sheet.

Brain Builder

Name_____

How do scientists help us?

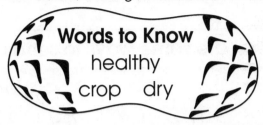
Words to Know
healthy
crop   dry

Helping Hands

George Washington Carver was a scientist. He studied peanuts. He found more than 300 ways to use them! Soap and ink are two things he made from peanuts. George studied other foods, too. He won a lot of awards for his hard work.

George liked to share what he learned. He helped farmers. He taught them how to make their soil healthy. He showed the farmers a lot of ways to use their crops. He told them how to dry and can their food, too. George did a lot of important work!

1. What was George's job? _____

2. **Look** back in the passage. **Underline** the sentence that lets you know people liked the work George did.

3. How do you know that George cared about people?

_____

_____

Brain Builder

Think about George's work. How might things be different today if he had not studied peanuts and other foods? Write your ideas on the back of this sheet.

What are some ways to send a message?

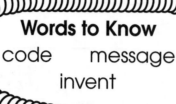

Words to Know

code   message

invent

Telephone Talk

A long time ago, there were no telephones. People used codes to send messages by fire or drums. It took a long time to send them. If a person did not know the code, he could not read the message. Then a man found a way to make sound go through wires. He used it to invent the phone.

Now a phone call is a fast way to talk to someone. We can talk to people who live far away. We can talk to people who live near us. We can call a friend. We can call for help. We can even call for pizza!

1. Do you think using fires or drums was a good way to send messages? Why or why not? _____

_____

2. **Look** back at the passage. **Underline** the sentence that tells how a phone works.

3. **Think** about the passage. How might a phone be helpful? **Draw** a picture to show your answer.

> Do you think the telephone is an important invention? Why or why not? Write your answer on the back of this sheet.

Brain Builder

Name _____

What do you know about bikes?

Words to Know
pedals
against
travel

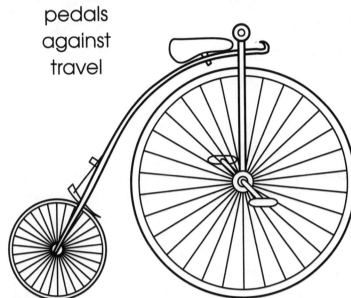

Bike Ride

Do you know that the first bike had no pedals? The rider pushed his feet against the road to make it go. Later a man made a new kind of bike. It had pedals and a big front wheel. The riders could travel much faster. People began to use bikes in place of horses.

Now people use bikes to get from place to place. They use bikes for exercise and fun, too!

1. **Complete** each sentence with a word from the passage.

   a. The first bike did not have _____.

   b. Pedals help bikes move _____.

2. **Circle** the word in the passage that tells how people traveled before they had bikes.

3. **Write** two reasons people use bikes.

   _____   _____

4. For each word below, **write** a word from the passage that means almost the same.

   a. street _____   b. go _____

Brain Builder

Which would you like better: to travel by bike or by horse? Write and explain your answer on the back of this sheet.

What do you know about television?

Television Over Time

It took a long time to invent the television. A lot of people worked on the idea. One of them was a boy in high school!

The first pictures on a TV screen were black and white. Now they can be in color. The first TV sets were small. Now they can be very big or small. Some TV sets are so small they can fit in a pocket! TV has changed the way we live. It helps us see what it is like in other parts of the world. It helps us find out news right away. It can even help us learn!

Words to Know
picture
screen
set

1. **Look** back at the passage. **Underline** the word that means the same as "made different."

2. **Circle** the word in the passage that means the same as "TV."

3. **Read** the sentences below. **Draw** a **+** in the box beside each one that is true.
   ☐ a. Many people helped invent the TV.
   ☐ b. Students cannot invent things.
   ☐ c. The first TV sets were not very big.

4. **Think** about the passage. **Write** one way that TV has changed.

_____

How might a TV help people learn? Write your ideas on the back of this sheet.

Brain Builder

©2000 The Education Center, Inc. • *Comprehension Connections* • TEC4112 • Key p. 64

Name_____

What do you know about the first Thanksgiving?

Words to Know
Pilgrims   crop
thanks

A Time to Give Thanks

Turkey, squash, and pie are on the table. A lot of people are here. It is November. It must be Thanksgiving!

The Pilgrims had the first Thanksgiving a long time ago. It was in <u>autumn</u>. It was a time for the Pilgrims to give thanks for good <u>crops</u>. They gave thanks for their new homes, too. The Pilgrims ate a <u>feast</u> with their Native American friends. Some of them played games. The <u>holiday</u> lasted for three days.

Now Thanksgiving is on the fourth Thursday in November. It lasts just one day, but it is still a lot of fun!

1. **Read** the words underlined in the passage. **Write** each one in the correct blank.

   a. a lot of food _____
   b. a day to celebrate _____
   c. fall _____
   d. plants _____

2. Why did the Pilgrims have Thanksgiving? _____

   _____

3. **Look** back in the passage. **Underline** the sentence that tells what some Pilgrims did for fun at the feast.

Brain Builder

How is Thanksgiving today like the first Thanksgiving? How is it different? Write your ideas on the back of this sheet.

Name _____

What does it mean to be curious?

Just Like Birds

Do you like to know how toys work? Orville and Wilbur Wright did! These brothers lived many years ago. They were curious. They liked to invent. The two men tried to find a way to fly like birds.

The Wright brothers worked a long time to make a plane with a motor. It was hard work. At last it was ready for them to ride. The plane stayed in the sky for 12 seconds. It went about as far as a person can throw a ball. The brothers were very happy. Now they knew how to fly like birds!

Words to Know
invent
motor
second

1. The Wright brothers made and fixed bikes in a store. **Think** about the passage. **Write** why this was a good job for them. _____

   _____

2. **Look** back in the passage. **Circle** the word that means "make something for the first time."

3. **Read** the sentences below. **Draw** an **X** in the box beside the sentence that tells what the story is mostly about.

   ☐ a. Orville and Wilbur Wright had a lot of toys.
   ☐ b. It is a lot of fun to fly in a plane.
   ☐ c. The Wright brothers made the first plane with a motor that could fly.

   The plane that Orville and Wilbur made did not go very far. Why do you think they were so happy about it?

   Brain Builder

What do you know about the Olympic® Games?

Go for the gold! That is what Jesse Owens did. When he was a boy, he was sick a lot. He ran to get stronger. The coach at school knew that Jesse could be a great runner. He helped Jesse run each day. Jesse got stronger and faster. When Jesse was older, he won a lot of races. He went to the Olympic® Games. He ran faster than anyone. He jumped farther than anyone. Jesse won four gold medals. That was the first time someone had won four medals at once. Jesse was a star!

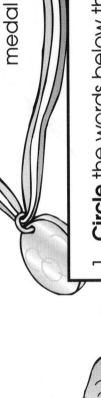

Words to Know

coach   gold

medal

1. **Circle** the words below that tell about Jesse. (*Hint: There are three of them.*)

   last   runner   lazy   fast   winner

2. **Look** back in the passage. **Underline** the sentence that tells what Jesse was like when he was young.

3. What does the author mean by "go for the gold"?

   _____

   _____

4. What is a good title for this passage? Why?

   _____

   _____

Brain Builder

On the back of this sheet, draw pictures to tell about Jesse's life. Make them look like a comic strip.

Name_____ *Graphic organizer*

At the Center!

Follow your teacher's directions to show what you read about.

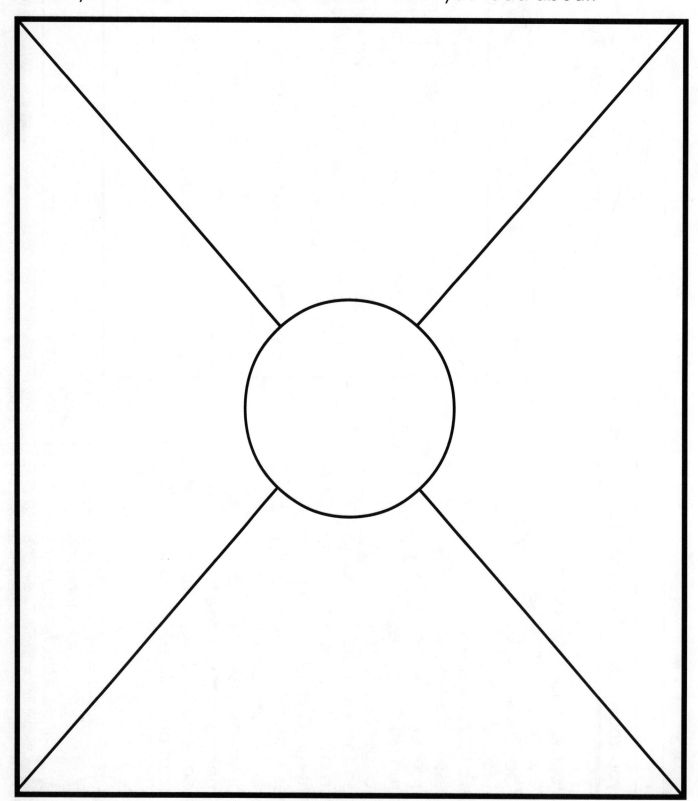

Note to the teacher: At the conclusion of a passage, give each student a copy of this sheet. The youngster writes the passage topic in the circle. In each remaining section, she writes a different word that relates to the topic and then uses it in a sentence. She adds an illustration for each one, if desired. Next, each youngster shares her work in a small group. Then a representative from each group tells the class about the similarities and differences among the group members' word choices.

Name

Topic Train

Hop aboard the Topic Train!
Follow your teacher's directions to tell about what you read.

I read about

Note to the teacher: After students finish reading a passage, give each youngster a copy of this sheet. Instruct him to complete the sentence on the train engine. Ask the student to write something he learned about the passage topic on each train car, referring to the passage as necessary. Then invite each youngster to share his work with a partner.

61

Answer Keys

Page 6
1. <u>All living things need air, food, and water.</u>
2. bugs, people, trees
3. a. yes
   b. no
   c. no

Brain Builder: Drawings will vary. Accept any reasonable responses. Written responses may vary but should include that living things need air, food, water, and (in most cases) sunlight.

Page 7
1. air, water, food
2. not living
3. a. no
   b. yes
   c. yes
   d. no

Brain Builder: Answers will vary. Possible answers include any two of the following: Living things need food, water, and air, but nonliving things do not.
Living things grow and change. Nonliving things do not grow, and they need help to change.
Living things can reproduce, but nonliving things cannot.

Page 8
1. a. care
   b. seeds
   c. learn
2. alone
3. Answers will vary but should include that people learn to eat, talk, and walk as they grow.

Brain Builder: Answers will vary. Accept any reasonable responses.

Page 9
1. the needs of plants
2. <u>sun</u> (yellow underline)
3. <u>soil</u> (brown underline)
4. air, water, food, light

Brain Builder: Posters will vary. They should each mention providing air, water, food, and light for the plant.

Page 10
1. Answers will vary. Accept any reasonable responses.
2. three
3. root (d), leaves (b), flower (a), stem (c)

Brain Builder: Answers will vary. Accept any reasonable responses.

Page 11
1. corn — stem
   carrot — seed
   lettuce — fruit
   celery — leaves
   apple — root

2. a. no
   b. yes
3. The foods should be colored as follows: corn (yellow), lettuce and celery (green), apple (red), carrot (orange).

Brain Builder: Accept any reasonable responses. Pictures will vary but should show that some plants are a source of food.

Page 12
1. a. <u>Whales</u> (blue underline)
   b. <u>Bats</u> (green underline)
   c. <u>Rabbits</u> (brown underline)
2. camel — North Pole
   polar bear — sky
   whale — desert
   bat — ocean

Brain Builder: Drawings and sentences will vary. Accept any reasonable responses.

Page 13
1. Answers will vary but should include that people need to be sure they can provide the type of care their pets would need.
2. water, love, shelter, food
3. Answers will vary. Accept any reasonable responses.

Brain Builder: Drawings and sentences will vary but should include water, love, shelter, and food.

Page 14
1. a. <u>ocean</u>
   b. large
2. mammal <u>whale</u>
   gills <u>fish</u>
   sideways fins <u>whale</u>
   egg <u>fish</u>
3. Answers may vary but should include that whales and fish are alike in many ways.

Brain Builder: Similarities may include that they live in the ocean and they have fins. Differences may include that fish have up-and-down tail fins and whales have sideways tail fins. Fish use gills to breathe, and whales go to the top of the water to breathe. Fish come from eggs, and whales are born alive.

Page 15
1. <u>They hear with small hairs on their bodies.</u>
2. a. no
   b. yes
   c. yes
3. Answers will vary. Accept any reasonable responses.

Brain Builder: Drawings and sentences will vary but should reflect common characteristics of insects, such as three body parts and six legs. Feelers may be included.

Page 16
1. <u>The egg is small. It might be as small as the top of a pin.</u>
2. starts — opens
   still — begins
   cracks — quiet
   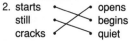
3. a. 2
   b. 1
   c. 4
   d. 3

Brain Builder: Drawings will vary but should reflect four stages in this order: egg, caterpillar, chrysalis, butterfly.

Page 17
1. queens, workers
2. worker
3. one
4. anthills
5. Answers will vary. Accept any reasonable responses.

Brain Builder: Answers will vary. Accept any reasonable responses.

Page 18
1. **reptiles**   **amphibians**
   scales   moist skin
   dry skin   eggs like jelly
   look like their parents   smooth
2. hard, soft
3. a. reptile
   b. amphibian

Brain Builder: Answers will vary. Accept any reasonable responses.

Page 19
1. Answers should include one of the following points: Neither frogs nor toads have tails. They do not chew their food. They both blink to push their food down. Most frogs and toads lay eggs.
2. a. chew
   b. long
   c. land
3. Most frogs have longer back legs than toads.

Brain Builder: Answers will vary. Accept any reasonable responses.

Page 20
1. a. no
   b. no
   c. yes
2. If a snake has fangs, it has poison.
3. a. legs
   b. swallow
4. harm
5. <u>whole</u>

Brain Builder: Answers will vary. Accept any reasonable responses.

Page 21
1. Accept any four of the following: <u>snow</u>, <u>cold</u>, <u>rains</u>, <u>sunny</u>, <u>windy</u>, <u>warm</u>, <u>calm.</u>
2. Answers may vary. Accept any reasonable responses.
3. The following words should each have a line drawn through them: garden, boat, flip-flops, work.

Brain Builder: Answers will vary. Accept any reasonable responses.

Page 22
1. rainy, cloudy, partly sunny, sunny
2. sunny
3. Answers will vary. Accept any reasonable responses.

Brain Builder: Answers will vary. Accept any reasonable responses.

Page 23

	rain	thunder	lightning	wind	spinning cloud	grows over an ocean
thunderstorm	+	+	+	+		
tornado	+	+	+	+	+	
hurricane	+	+	+	+	+	+

Brain Builder: The hurricane is the wildest because it can have tornadoes and thunderstorms with it. (Answers may vary. Accept any reasonable responses.)

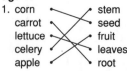

Answer Keys

Page 24
1. a. You are eating lunch
   b. You are sleeping.
   c. You are watching for shooting stars.
   d. You are leaving school in the afternoon.
2. You cannot feel it spin.
3. Answers will vary. Accept any reasonable responses.
Brain Builder: Pictures will vary. Accept any reasonable responses.

Page 25
1. a. + (Sentences b and c should not be marked.)
2. a. 3   c. 4
   b. 2   d. 1
Brain Builder: The moon does not die. We cannot see the moon when the sun does not shine on it. (Answers may vary. Accept any reasonable responses.)

Page 26
1. heat, light
2. The sun looks as if it is the largest star because it is the closest star to the earth.
3. Answers will vary but should include that there would be no life.
4. a. miles
   b. hot
   c. car
Brain Builder: Answers will vary. Accept any reasonable responses.

Page 27
1. what a body needs to be healthy
2. Accept any one of the following: eat good foods, get plenty of rest, exercise, or keep clean.
3. a. germs   c. healthy
   b. exercise   d. heart
Brain Builder: Drawings and explanations will vary. Accept any reasonable responses.

Page 28
1. fruits, meats, beans, cheese
2. a. energy
   b. fat
   c. Food
3. a. yes
   b. yes
   c. no
Brain Builder: Answers will vary. Accept any answer similar to the following: I might not have enough energy to run, play, or read a book.

Page 29
1. candy, cake, cookies, soda
2. a. Cavities are holes in your teeth.
   b. Milk (or cheese) makes teeth healthy.
3. Brushing gets food and germs off your teeth.
Brain Builder: Posters will vary. Accept any reasonable responses.

Page 30
1. a. yes   d. yes
   b. yes   e. no
   c. no
2. weight
3. dull
4. Answers will vary. They may include that all things are made of matter and that matter takes up space and has weight.
Brain Builder: Drawings will vary. Sentences should include that the things take up space and have weight.

Page 31
1. Answers may vary but should include that they are both states of matter.
2. Answers may vary but should include that a solid has its own shape and a gas has no shape.
3. a. liquid ⟶ has no shape
   b. solid ⟶ can be poured
   c. gas ⟶ has its own shape
4. solid, liquid, gas
Brain Builder: Answers will vary. Accept any reasonable responses.

Page 32
1. a. float
   b. sink
   c. push
2. a. sink
   b. float
3. They push away enough water.
Brain Builder: Answers will vary but should reflect that the best way is to test it because it can be hard to guess whether something will sink or float.

Page 33
1. a. home ⟶ not the same
   b. different ⟶ not many
   c. few ⟶ place to live
   d. dry ⟶ not wet
2. The stilts keep their homes high and dry.
3. b. There are many different kinds of homes.
Brain Builder: Heavy snow cannot break strong roofs.

Page 34
1. a. fruits
   b. rice
   c. potatoes
2. a. Fruits grow in places that are hot. (red underline)
   b. Rice grows in places that are very wet. (blue underline)
3. This passage is about the foods people grow and eat in different places.
Brain Builder: Answers will vary but should include thinking about the area and its typical weather.

Page 35
1. a. ice hockey
   b. soccer
2. forest
3. The weather and the places they live affect what they can do outside for fun.
Brain Builder: Answers will vary. Accept any reasonable responses.

Page 41
1.
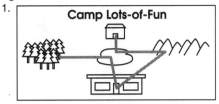
2. a. The map helps Sam ⟶ has a key.
   b. Every map ⟶ find places.
   c. A key tells us ⟶ trips.
   d. People can use maps to plan ⟶ about the map pictures.
Brain Builder: Some people might not know what the pictures mean.
(Answers will vary. Accept any reasonable responses.)

Page 36
1. a. The schools had few books.
   b. slates
2. Accept any three of the following: books, paper, pencils, crayons, computers.
3. Answers will vary. Accept any reasonable responses. Possibilities include the following: Schools long ago had only one room, but now schools have many. Students of many different ages were taught together long ago, but now students usually have classmates who are about the same age. Today schools have a lot more books and supplies than they did long ago.
Brain Builder: Answers will vary. Accept any reasonable responses.

Page 37
1. horses, mules, oxen
2. Answers will vary. Accept any reasonable responses.
3. plane, bus, car
4. Answers will vary. Accept any reasonable responses.
Brain Builder: Answers will vary. Accept any reasonable responses.

Page 38
1. chores
2. cook, sew
3. Answers may include any two of the following: sticks, string, rocks, leaves.
4. Pioneer homes did not have running water. The pioneers needed to get their water from places such as rivers or ponds.
Brain Builder: The children were tired at night because they worked and played hard.

Page 39
1. b. A city is a large community and a town is a small one.
2. X a lot of tall buildings
   X a lot of cars and buses
   X a large community
   X a lot of stores
3. No, a town would have fewer stores and schools because a town has fewer people than a city.
Brain Builder: Answers will vary. Accept any reasonable responses.

Page 40
1.

Mountains	Ocean
hike	jump the waves
snow-ski	swim
climb rocks	write in the sand

2. All people cannot go rock climbing because not everyone lives by the mountains.
3. Answers will vary. Accept any reasonable responses.
Brain Builder: Pictures will vary. Accept any reasonable responses.

Answer Keys

Page 42
1. food, clothing, shelter
2. Wants are things you would like to have but can live without.
3. a. no
   b. yes
   c. yes
   d. no

Brain Builder: Drawings will vary. Accept any reasonable responses.

Page 43
1. Goods are things that people make and then sell. (blue underline)
2. A service is a job that someone is paid to do. (red underline)
3. a. no
   b. yes
   c. yes
4. teaching
   driving a bus
   cars
   flowers
   fixing cars

Brain Builder: Drawings will vary. Accept any reasonable responses.

Page 44
1. ± The cost will go up.
   ± The toy will be hard to find.
2. demand, supply, cost

Brain Builder: Drawings will vary. Accept any reasonable responses.

Page 45
1. neighbors
2. a. belongs to
   b. shares
   c. litter
3. x a. follows the rules
   x c. takes good care of his math book

Brain Builder: Answers will vary. Accept any reasonable responses.

Page 46
1. + a.
   + c.
2. a. need
   b. right
   c. citizens

Brain Builder: Answers will vary. Accept any reasonable responses.

Page 47
1. a. follow
   b. home
   c. community
   d. safe
2. If she watches TV before she starts her homework, she might not have enough time to finish her work.
3. Answers will vary. Accept any reasonable responses.

Brain Builder: Answers will vary. Accept any reasonable responses.

Page 48
1. floors
2. more than 75
3. bowl
4. Answers will vary but should refer to the oval shape. Accept any reasonable responses.

Brain Builder: Answers will vary. Accept any reasonable responses.

Page 49
1. Answers will vary. Accept any reasonable responses.
2. America
3. July 4 or the Fourth of July
4. X b.

Brain Builder: Answers will vary. Accept any reasonable responses.

Page 50
1. a. yes
   b. no
   c. no
2. There is one star for every state in the United States.
3. Answers will vary. Accept any reasonable responses.

Brain Builder: Answers will vary. Accept any reasonable responses.

Page 51
1. kind, president, smart, speaker
2. a. yes
   b. no
   c. no
   d. yes
3. Answers will vary. Accept any reasonable responses.

Brain Builder: Answers will vary. Accept any reasonable responses.

Page 52
1. unfair
2. Rosa Parks went to jail because the law said that she was supposed to stand if there were no more seats for white people. She would not stand.
3. 2, 1, 4, 3

Brain Builder: Answers will vary. Accept any reasonable responses.

Page 53
1. George was a scientist.
2. He won a lot of awards for his hard work.
3. He shared what he learned. He helped people.

Brain Builder: Answers will vary. Accept any reasonable responses.

Page 54
1. Answers will vary. Accept any reasonable responses.
2. Then a man found a way to make sound go through wires.
3. Drawings will vary. Accept any reasonable responses.

Brain Builder: Answers will vary. Accept any reasonable responses.

Page 55
1. a. pedals
   b. faster
2. horses
3. Answers will vary. Accept any reasonable responses.
4. a. road
   b. travel

Brain Builder: Answers will vary. Accept any reasonable responses.

Page 56
1. changed
2. television
3. + a.
   + c.
4. Accept either of the following: Televisions can now have color pictures. Televisions can be either big or small.

Brain Builder: Answers will vary. Accept any reasonable responses.

Page 57
1. a. feast
   b. holiday
   c. autumn
   d. crops
2. They had Thanksgiving to give thanks for good crops and new homes.
3. Some of them played games.

Brain Builder: Answers will vary. Accept any reasonable responses.

Page 58
1. They liked to know how things worked. They liked to make things. (Answers may vary. Accept any reasonable responses.)
2. invent
3. X c.

Brain Builder: Answers may vary but should include that the brothers had worked very hard and were pleased to see that their invention worked.

Page 59
1. runner, fast, winner
2. When he was a boy, he was sick a lot.
3. Answers will vary but should include trying to succeed.
4. Answers will vary. Accept any reasonable responses.

Brain Builder: Drawings will vary, but the events of Jesse's life that they depict should be in sequence.